Naked In Daylight

Naked In Daylight

Carol Adler, MFA

A Dandelion Books Publication
www.dandelion-books.com

Copyright, 2010, by Carol Adler

All rights exclusively reserved. No part of this book may be reproduced or translated into any language or utilized in any form or by any means, electronic or mechanical, including photocopying, recording or by any information storage and retrieval system, without permission in writing from the publisher.

Dandelion Books, LLC
Mesa, Arizona

Adler, Carol: Naked in Daylight – Poems by Carol Adler
   ISBN 978-1-934280-86-7
   LC Number - 2010940374

Ebook Edition – First Published - May 2008
   ISBN 978-1-934280-62-1, 1-934280-62-3

Cover & Interior Design by Accurance.com

Disclaimer and Reader Agreement

This is a work of poetry. Any resemblance of fictional characters in this book to living or deceased individuals is purely coincidental. Neither the author nor the publisher, Dandelion Books, LLC, shall be liable for any damages or costs related to any coincidental resemblances of the fictional characters in this book to living or deceased individuals. Under no circumstances will the publisher, Dandelion Books, LLC, or author be liable to any person or business entity for any direct, indirect, special, incidental, consequential, or other damages based on any use of this book or any other source to which it refers, including, without limitation, any lost profits, business interruption, or loss of programs or information.

Dandelion Books, LLC
www.dandelion-books.com

Solitude

my jealous lover:

say you need me.

CONTENTS

FOREWORD: AFTER CATULLUS xi

PROXIMITY OF PERCEPTION 1
    The Significance of Conversation 3
  Pre-Natal 5
    Tear Up the Contract and Start Walking 6
    Belief Systems 7
    Addict 8
    Life of One Saint 9
    Another World 10
    Today's Special 12
    Displacement Myth: Electrophotography, or The Tree
        Inside Each Acorn 14
    The Right Communication 16
    Wilber in Broad Daylight 17
    Retired Colonel 18
    Elijah 20
    Conversion 22
    Proximity of Perception 23
    The Appraiser 24

THE MASTERY OF LOVE 27

    If Good Doesn't Come 25

    Roses 31

    Truth is a Lie Not Yet Formed 32

    Transformation 33

    What Then? 34

    Away 36

    One Day 37

    Crow-Eating: Male, White, Southern 39

    Unconditional 41

    Altered State 43

    The Mastery of Love 45

    Trusting 47

    Homebody 49

    After Making Love 50

TEA AT THE EVERGLADES BATH & TENNIS CLUB 51

    Jet Path 53

    Malaise 54

    Tea at the Everglades Bath & Tennis Club 55

WEATHERING 57

    Inhuman Needs 59

    The Reason for Metaphor 61

    Age of Uncovery: April Fool's Day 63

    Fourth of July 66

    October Moon 69

    Attracting Opposites 71

LEAVING 73

    It Was a Leveling 75

    Leaving 77

    Locking the Door Open 78

    No One 81

    You, Silence 82

    Remnant 83

    Rishea 84

    Carte Blanche 86

    Dream 87

    Lies 91

    Gifts 93

THANK YOU 95

    Thank You 97

    Agenda 99

    It's Only a Matter of 102

    Beauty in the Eyes of the Beholder 104

    Song: "Occasional Times" 106

ONE-LETTER WORD 109
    One-Night Stop 111
    River of Blood 114
    One Letter Word 116
    Cinema Paridiso 123
    Sleeping Planet 124
    The Most Profound of All Messages 127
    Displaced 129
    Naked in Daylight 130

CAROL ADLER 131

FOREWORD

AFTER CATULLUS

I have no problem
sharing this extraordinary
collection of
rhetorical gems because
I know the
whole world has been
waiting
for them

PROXIMITY OF PERCEPTION

THE SIGNIFICANCE OF CONVERSATION

In the current condition, even before two people meet, they can dissolve or slip through the keyhole. Only the other day a woman tried to act as an impostor and got framed as the whore who called herself Little Bo Peep at the topless bar next to the airport. When she screamed that her credibility was at stake, they tied her to a cash register and tested her breath, three officers taking turns. This insult drove her to rent a husband who was a catfish farmer currently in the business of digging sinkholes. But the plan backfired. He fell for her head over heels, and she inherited neither fish nor farm.

A century or so went by. Then one day in broad daylight down the street from KFC and Wendy's, Gamaliel was in the rest room reading the comics and he came across a strip called Mother Goose. There she was, plucking feathers and singing nursery rhymes to Little Dell. He rang her immediately to introduce himself as a Doctor of Jewish Law, and she married him without even checking his cholesterol.

Complacency tends to get lost like socks in the dryer, so we'll skip over the years and come to the immediate dialogue: "How lucky you are to have hair." He didn't respond so she tried again. "Does it bother you to talk?"

"Only once, when I was a child," he replied. "Of course you understand."

In vain, Bo Peep searched for a straw, but the restaurant had just been invaded by a busload of fanatics on their way to The Falls. Reaching into her bra, she pulled out the one she'd saved from a previous shake. "It'll do," straightening it. "No," changing her mind. It wasn't clean and the tip was lipsticked… but she certainly couldn't use her *mouth*.

PRE-NATAL

My cosmetics had been stolen and
my body was in pain. Part of
me had forgotten to turn off the
alarm but it was too late the bombing had begun
my shoes were too tight and when I opened my
mouth the streets shriveled up; with my iron I
immediately set to work straightening
corners. At this point it didn't matter if the
post office was locked because the message was
clear: this was my chance. Even the red ink had
risen in the neck of my goose, my crotch itched
and my hands fell away from all credentials as naturally
as if I'd never been stamped.
Never before had I ever been so sure of the
odor of run. Here at last, like Christmas seals on December's
bills was His Mistress' Voice
crooning out of the ducts…: "Iiiiiiyyyiiiiiim dreeeeeeam-ing…"

Carol Adler

TEAR UP THE CONTRACT AND START WALKING

This is my proclamation delivered at the stroke of indecision just before the twelfth hole at a moment that has never occurred. It's time for Laura to examine her parts to find out where they belong; she must either make peace with them and tell them where to go or hire a man. And June needs to find an addiction, she can't go on forever expecting others to look the other way every time she caters their affairs. Anyway, she's too good a cook to be wasted on grits. The stomachs here are waving their flags, the toilets are turning green, Morley's dreams are collecting dust in the delivery room, Dick's Toby Mugs are growing tails. I can no longer afford to rent my clothes nor can I willingly recycle my unclaimed fears, which means it's finally time to separate visions from glass.

All this left-brain thinking as I awoke by accident and discovered myself seated at the head of the class waiting for adjournment. First, however, I knew I would be asked to say something blue, which would definitely be against all tradition and would never match with my closing stanza. What should I do?

Fortunately my recorder was hitched up to the dust directly behind me, so I immediately dictated a dozen revisions.

BELIEF SYSTEMS

"What do you want for my life?" shrieked the old man in shorts who dyed his hair orange. As pedestrians hustled by close enough to be mugged, he began to wonder who really was worthy enough to be a victim. After all, he wasn't getting any younger and the world was growing colder and warmer by the minute.

At the corner beneath an umbrella, a yellow-haltered woman with a red ponytail was painting hot-dogs. Around her neck was a Star of David that didn't really mean anything, she lied.

A long white limousine splashed mud on the man's trousers, and as he lurched back from the curb, his left foot landed in a mustardy nest of dogshit. In court we learned the driver was a dog with his dead mother in the back seat.

When the umbrella collapsed, the woman's wig fell off. On her shaved head was a Star of David.

ADDICT

Yesterday a whole fried chicken strutted into the patio and ignoring the knocker, pounded on the door, demanding reasons. How had he guessed I'd just nested a dozen eggs in my right brain next to the vacuum? "Intuition," he shouted. Hot bubbles sizzled out of his angry balloon and I could taste the grit; my stomach gurgled. "Please," I begged, "right now I can't fit you in." "Ahh, so *that's* it!" His comb bristled as he stepped out of his crust and lunged. "Time!" he roared, capturing me by the books. "And Life," I squawked as he swung me around as if *shlagging kapparos*.[1] I watched the grease pour from his balls, watched my precious poems curl and shrivel into salty strips. Brusquely, he picked each one up, crumbled them in his fist, belched and sprinkled them into his wingpits. "Please, I have no insurance." His grip tightened. "Good; then make a wish." He clucked and grinned as he studied my wrists, deliberating which one to break first.

---

[1] *Shlagging Kapparos* is an annual custom performed by many Jews on Erev Yom Kippur (Yom Kippur Eve). One takes a live chicken and swings it over one's head three times while saying a Hebrew phrase to the effect that this chicken should be slaughtered in lieu of oneself who may be deserving of like punishment for sins committed throughout the year.

LIFE OF ONE SAINT

"When he fished for compliments he ended up throwing them back because he felt unworthy," said the eulogist, helping himself to more scrod and parsleyed potatoes.

"He was cruising down the Interstate when he got bumped off by two sharks looking for shit," the sheriff wiped his mouth on his sleeve. "'You got the wrong guy, I ain't got nothin',' he said. I s'pose there ain't nothin' wrong with provin' he was right for once. He did have nothin', 'cept maybe the skin an' bones that was his life. So for a stiff fee I let him go. What goes around comes around. We need a new jail."

Personal friends requested that parking fees be waived. In front, diapers flapped on the flag pole and by the urinal one of the cousins was selling condoms from the Holy Land.

"He wasn't a bad man, but he wasn't a good one, either," sighed his mother, clutching his teeth in her fist. "That's OK," said the priest. "That's enough to put down, you can charge the rest."

Carol Adler

ANOTHER WORLD

They were eating Chinese and discussing
the stock market, five of them. Each
a different order now undone, seated
amidst clutters of domes and bowls.

"The economy stinks," said the lawyer, helping
himself to more pork. In the center of
the table, orange wax flickered
in its lotus-shaped glass.

"What's the problem?" asked his wife, digging
into her sweet-and-sour shrimp.
"You mean what's new?" added Ken, a writer
who worked for the local paper. He liked
beef and the usual, which looked like
chow mein. Mixed aromas
of incense and fry. Heavy perfume.
Toujours Moi? Paco Rabonne? "I just had an
abortion," whispered Ann, Ken's daughter, to her
new stepmother, June. June smiled benignly
as she picked at her lobster with a foreign name.
She was glad her dress matched the orange of the

candle, glad she was wearing pearls.
Glad she liked her new husband and that
he also liked to Go Chinese.

"Isn't it a good thing?" she remarked, helping
herself to more rice. The waiter poured
the tea and wondered why there was no
steam. He wished he could say more than
Yes. Please. Without a smile. **Thank you.**

Carol Adler

TODAY'S SPECIAL

As if it were Birdland or the Boardwalk
or just Octogenarian Day at the market
in their shiny rubber-wheeled toys they rudder
themselves into the parking lot
and as soon as the doors open fly in
first to the toilets
then to sample handouts squeeze
grapefruits prod melons.

Today is Free Weigh-In. One by
one they line up and bounce on the scales

but the needle's wrong i'm too fat too thin
just right just right osteoporosis osteoporosis

Lettuce is up cucumbers are down
"This is a tomato?" shouts Becky. "Fire one!"
"PLAY BALL PLAY BALL!" shouts Nathan in
Bermuda shorts and cap, aiming an apple
at his wife.

"Cottage cheese cottage cheese," chirps pinafored
Caroline, lifting each lid and peeking inside.
"I WILL smoke if I WANT TO," shouts Harvey
blowing a mouthful in the manager's face.
"Happy Birthday, Hon," shrieks Dolores in Bakery
sticking her finger in a chocolate cake.

whadda ya want tanight the same old
i'm sicka yer stale yer salty yer tasteless
and you know what you can do with yer goddamn greasy
I HATE SPINACH GODDAMMIT
a tisket a tasket
junkfood for my basket

"How will it end?" asks Gladys on Register Eight.
"Probably a blood bath," shrugs her packer.
But when? wonders Gabriel in Aisle Seven
mopping up eggs milk yogurt sour cream antiseptic

Carol Adler

DISPLACEMENT MYTH: ELECTROPHOTOGRAPHY, OR, THE TREE INSIDE EACH ACORN

Semyon Kirlian took a photograph
of his eye
and discovered the eye
known as Semyon Kirlian
staring back at him.

He blinked at the two eyes
but only one blinked back. He winked
with his left eye. Semyon the
photograph crumpled and
bent left. He put on
a Jane Fonda workout tape.
The eye put on a silvery leotard
and waited for Jane to
begin. But this was the advanced
program without warm-ups.
Semyon was a heavy man and
was already snockered on
vodka. "What's
the problem?" asked
Jane, stripping to the waist.

"My perception," moaned
Semyon, blinking nervously.
His eye swelled with
vision as Jane's hair
fell into his face in a shower
of tigers. "Copy me,"
she ordered. "Copy me,"
panted Semyon.

"Harder," she commanded. God, this
was great. Semyon obeyed.

Jane winked at him.

Semyon's eye popped out of the
DVD and started to crack up.
"Careful!" warned Jane,
too late.

Carol Adler

THE RIGHT COMMUNICATION

A lipstick rolls out of the mirror and turns left on Universal Boulevard just in time to watch all the bitten off fingernails grow long enough to be alphabetized. Outside, water purrs indifferently past strolling hot dogs ribboned and ringed, still looking for the right brain even though frustration is already stacking chairs and counting the cash. How can anyone know what to say without asking first—as if books could kill, like names and sticks—or know when not to be spontaneous and congenital?

Taking a cue from the gathering harbor, all the medium-size bowling balls hustle into their uniforms and line up as an affront to the approaching calibration. The array of guilt is remarkable, observes a visiting reporter. There's nothing to feel, writes another. And as we survey the venders and count the prisoners, this seems to be the case. (If only we could sell our illusions and settle for ongoing propriety with no problems except maybe an hourly bell and occasional whimper.)

Inside, the pool fills with stars even though the evening is still missing. "No problem," purred the operator to her glowing laptop.

WILBER IN BROAD DAYLIGHT

Wilber spent ten years at a seminary
pretending to be celibate, and ended up
marrying Sebastian because he had to. After six
rhythm babies out of wed-
lock, Bible class twice a week and
confession every Sunday, Sebastian fell
in love with a lesbian security
officer at the factory where he assembled
mannequins. "I love Marty for his tits and
buns," moaned Sebastian at Sunday confessional.

"No small matter," said the
priest, shaking incense
over Sebastian's buns. "This will
take care of everything."
He was right. Marty swapped his uniform for
one without tits, Wilber became a
nun and every Sunday Sebastian paid a Catholic
mannequin to confess to the priest.

Carol Adler

RETIRED COLONEL

"It's time for tea," says the lamb,
blotting his saliva with her
pen and adjusting the forget-
me-nots to catch the sun.

But the Colonel has to pee first.
"It's like this all day," he mutters.
"With so many demands, it's impossible
to fill in all the blanks without
a dictionary. Eat, sleep
and pee, no four-letter
words and nothing beginning
with 'W' except wait, what, want,
wort went…"

"The President is on Line Four," squeaks
Mousie, removing his bubble
and handing him a wand. "He
says he can't do anything about the grape
requisition and oreos until you
find the right line."

"Shit!" The Colonel pushes away

his troops as if they were merely the

head on a beer, bolts upright

and slides into his zipper.

He's sick of covering up. It's

time for some action. Why

couldn't He make His *own* sandwiches?

ELIJAH

When he roared through the door puffing
      on a cigar and waving coupons for
kosher soap, Grandpa dialed 911.
      "Smoking is not allowed," barked Grandma,
dousing his butt. The baby screamed
      "Oy Vey," Mama's wig vibrated, and Cousin,
who was gay, squeaked "this isn't funny."
      "Vulgar," agreed Niece, a freshman
at Harvard. "Who invited him?"
      "Roger, we must remember," whispered
Deputy Moss to Grandpa. "Come in, come in!"
      Grandma yanked out a wish bone from her
ear and shook it three times to the
      left, three times to the
right. "He could be Albert Einstein, or
      Marcel Proust," suggested Prodigy from
the crib. "Who's to know?" mourned
      Uncle, a permanent victim.

Meanwhile, Elijah was examining
      the wine spots on the cloth.
Then he opened
      his kit and took out
a miracle spot
      remover. "Next year it'll be
on the temple," he said
      before taking off.

Carol Adler

CONVERSION

Yesterday according to the sign on the steeple, the white A-frame village church became a jewelry store. The table in front is laden with glass diamonds, ice tongs, electric woks and walkmen. Inside under glass: picture frames and silver wish bones... at the far end, in green fluorescence, a speaker plays rock and a girl with foreign eyelashes and nails chews baseballs while she strokes the habit of a nun. Her body is glass with a plastic head. On TV at the cemetery the store is featured in a 30-second ad. "God is glitz," says the actor. By late afternoon the air smells of dog shit and tutti-frutti. "We were all Pilgrims once," preaches the minister.

PROXIMITY OF PERCEPTION

On the day his dog Spot ran away, Charles shaved off
his beard and cleaned up the pad. Just
as he opened the oven door to clear out his
rage, it blew up in his face. On the way to
the hospital his heart wouldn't start. The
closest neighbor was on valium and couldn't find
her clitoris so he walked two miles in ninety
degree heat to the last resort where he found
Spot eating crow with his former wife Joy.
Both under the influence, they didn't see
him coming.

"Joy, Joy," he called. Finally Spot trotted
over and started to bark Beethoven's "Ode to
Joy." "Celebrate!" shouted Charles.
"What?" muttered Joy, tearing up the electric
bill. Spot picked up the pieces, and like a
good dog chewed them back together.

On the spur of the moment, Charles realized he
was me, so I don't blame myself for driving her
crazy. Guiltlessly, I can call the shrink to ask if I can join
them for a little pleasure, who could ask for anything less?

Carol Adler

THE APPRAISER

I make appraisals.
I do mostly ocean estates.
It's easy to make money for
wealthy people. The ocean
knows me well.

When I went to one of Mike's hotels
that he's breaking up into condos
I worked on one with thick
carpets and wedding pictures on the piano.
I stood on the balcony and watched the
tide going out. I pretend I

have family. And a beautiful wife.
On the coffee table is a dish of
candy, one piece wouldn't be missed.
And by the telephone, a penny. In the
realtors' envelope is an extra twenty

(they don't usually give tips).
I'm often lonely
but I don't like to think about it.

Gloria the choir director once said I was an angel.
No one but me and Gloria know that.

I did a free appraisal for her and her man.
Her man's in a wheelchair, no legs.
Gloria's an angel, too.

Sometimes I wish I could die.

He was a pilot in Viet Nam, he said.

THE MASTERY OF LOVE

IF GOOD DOESN'T COME

What is love? asks a child,
her sick kitten cradled
in her arm.

Bedtime and snowstorms, steamy baths,
sleet tapping against the window, prickly as
Uncle Wiggley's bunny whiskers, my
father patiently saying yes
to another story I already knew by
heart. Propped up on one elbow at
the foot of the bed, he was the child,
I the kitten curled up in the soft
drone of his voice. Last time
I visited him in the nursing home, his eyes
filled as he said, "I want to help
you."

Finicky about daily shaves,
he says the barber's name
is Tom Someone
with six grandchildren and photos.
"Whiskers are only for creatures that
wiggle their ears," he

Carol Adler

grins, pressing my hand.
In *The Republic* Socrates masks as Plato and pretends
to know The Good. I got my
'A' but can only remember the professor's
beer belly and mismatched socks. My father
didn't need a course.

When he dies, I won't ask questions or
make statements, but take my place by
his workbench while he patiently hammers
tiny nails into leather sandals for my
Shirley Temple doll, each *tap-tap!*
a dotted exclamation poking out of
wintry fields like frosticled
bunny whiskers.

ROSES

They used to spend hours weeding
horseshoes, triangles and circles
planted mostly with roses.

Although I lived next door I didn't know
they were blind until I brought
them an American Beauty
for Christmas.

What was it about roses, I wondered,
the blooms glimmering in the green
like a watery Monet.

Even when it rained they were out there
weeding. Like monkeys in yellow slickers.

Carol Adler

TRUTH IS A LIE NOT YET FORMED

In a wet bathing suit I crouch in the corner of my misunderstanding. Terrified my stomach might discover it's stuck between floors in a jammed elevator, my body shivers its will to survive. My eyes lock shut, voices festering.

Don't tell me again about Mozart. Don't tell me I can't ever again experience the sensuousness of gold shimmering on my hips, words weaving their arms into garments of sex, fur-lined cloaks. Don't tell me I can't rip them off.

By the manhole, the police wait with teargas.
If I control myself, they'll know I'm scared.
If I shout, I turn myself in. Don't tell me
about love, how its needles poison the flesh and

spray paint messages on lavatory doors. Impotent because I
know everything and knowledge spreads,
I'm ready to confess I was never a virgin.

TRANSFORMATION

Like a parent teasing a child with candy
my lover tells me sex is evil.

Meanwhile, the cover is off
and I can smell the sin beneath
the foil.

Once in a moment of
weakness he almost said
he loved me.

Then, as if knowing my reply
could be more addictive than sugar
he snatched them back.

Afterward, he kissed me sweetly
on the tip of my nose.

Now I understand the meaning of guilt
and forgive myself
for counting the days until Christmas.
My lover was right.
For him, sex is evil.

Carol Adler

WHAT THEN?

I didn't come here to see the scar on his left
thigh, momento from the bar fight when he
threatened to kill me and I picked up a
knife. Large-bellied, reeking of skunk
and critter, one eye patched, the other
swollen—"What, then?" he grins, already
knowing. It's been like this all my
life. I go along thinking my goals are everyone's.
Strolling in the park, feeding ducks, or floating
through the Belvedere, bathing in Klimpt and
Schiele, in the afternoon nibbling pastries
at Aida or Dehmel's. Then I wake up lying in a litter
of greasy McDonald's wrappers
or in a Victorian garden, a bullet in my
chest, red-faced Adam
standing over me with his usual
accusation.

Or I'm writhing at the bottom of a
pit where I'm supposed to wait for
the rug dealers or used car salesman.
It's not that I ask for all
these myths I keep bumping

into. Who is this man who claims to be my
father, wife, brother, Atlantean cousin who does
mail orders on Herkimer crystals and Hong Kong
radionics?

I can't even get
rid of childhood traumas that never
happened, like getting locked in the
outhouse at Canandaigua Lake, or kidnapped
at Disneyland. I can still taste the
naphtha, feel the panic burning my
chest.

"We do belong together." Is he a four-
leaf clover I pressed into *Rebecca of Sunny-
brook Farm?* Cookie cutter I dumped in
the sand box when it was time for lunch, the
thundering bookcase I called God?
I lie under the full
moon waiting to get pregnant. Slimy with
sweat, his breath reeking of garlic, he
leans over me, studying the map.

Carol Adler

AWAY

Beneath the pile of broken promises
he glanced up at me from the bottom rung:
"I need you desperately."

His eyes were glazed
and I was a slave again,
carving his name in the wind.

And when we'd chased each other
from one world into the next
and he'd captured me, spinning me around
until I was dizzy and sure

he'd beg
from the bottom rung—
"I need you desperately."

His eyes would gloss over as one by
one the promises flew off

like bricks.

ONE DAY

"Nobody is, in effect, a perfectly good woman."
          —*Stealing the Language,* by Alice Suskin Ostriker

The strange thing was
I didn't know I was being punished
until my nipples shrieked
and I wanted them to be
twisted and pounded non-stop.

He could have poked
out my eyes
peeled me like an orange
peed on me.

What had I done
to deserve this pleasure?
Because he didn't know either,
he stopped, unmounted me

and strode away.
Now I write him letters
telling him it wasn't his fault,
but he doesn't answer.

Carol Adler

No wonder fortune-telling
is the growing trend
for those who refuse
to be superstitious.

CROW-EATING, MALE, WHITE, SOUTHERN

Honey Ah loves you like a frien
an you've got ta unnerstan
Ah've got lots uv acquaint'n'ses
but when it comes to friens—

cuz y'see Ah believe in pleasin
evraone
now mah firs wahf she tells me she say
she *lahked* ta be beaten
an ah swear ah coulda *killed* her sometahm
fer wantin ta be so stubbern

she was the bane a' mah good intenchuns
moral all raht
not a crooked bone in her skull

an when she done somethin
whatever it was
yawl can be damn sure it was done raht
no twistin aroun in *her* mahnd.
Fer *her* D' Trut' was D'Trut'.

Carol Adler

So when she took a gun an shot herself
Ah sweah All's Ah said to her
only jus the minute before Ah says
like Ah says to you now

"Honey Ah loves you like a frien—"

UNCONDITIONAL

Because I believe in love, I am here to
forgive the mother who stuffed
rage in my throat, the father who scalded my tongue
and lopped off my fingers. Here to embrace
the husband who raped and robbed me of dignity
and hope. Here to embrace the man who
flashed naked out of the bushes,
the men who knocked me to the ground and ran
off with my money, the men who trade lies
for sex, the men who call me man-hater
then beat me up, the men who come
to me with their amateur scripts, asking
for handouts.

I am especially here to forgive the man who
told me I was depressed.

My mother stands over me with a seven-
branched candleabra. My father feebly reaches
out and tries to remember me.
In a hospital gown, my husband
rises from his nightmare to greet me.
Prisoners wait for me to come. I place

Carol Adler

my clitoris on their tongues and force

their fear to melt into trust.

All night long I give the disempowered

my ripened vineyards, my

song of songs.

ALTERED STATE

I was lying next to a man who wanted to
make love to me and thinking about lying next
to my former husband by the swimming pool at
Ramat Gan. We were on our honeymoon and my husband, a
composer, was telling me about the time the
Hitler Youth tried to drown him.
I'll teach you how to swim, I promised. I didn't
say then that faith, not music, was the
universal language. I didn't urge him to
accept my offer, or even believe in me. Nor
would I have told him, ever, that his
father, who died young of cancer, had
also tried to drown him in cruel expectations
that could never be met. I had faith that
in time he would learn to let love be his
ballast. We made love,
I loved, oh I loved, and taught him how
to swim, but he never liked the water.

This man was sleek and tanned, every part of
him languaging desire. *I don't understand
propositions,* I protested coyly. *You don't have to,*
he grinned, *when love is unconditional.*

Indeed, I marveled, realizing now
it was not the sun but a hand on my
forehead, and again
there was music, wood flutes
and drums. But as soon as I said yes I
discovered myself floating in a cart through the
supermarket. Just ahead a
broom had fallen down, forcing me to detour
through baby food and diapers. Near the
nipples a crown of mistletoe dropped onto
my lips and I felt myself lifting into the
air on the strings of the third movement
of the Mahler 5th. The drums grew louder as the
flutes blew out morning glories in pastels that
matched the colors of the bathroom.

Yes, I repeated to the repair person
as he pulled out my
skull from the freezer. You're right.
It *is* time for a trade-in.

THE MASTERY OF LIFE

Every time she tried to learn
where she was

he came to her as direction.
From whence the source?

Let's start over.

A woman writes a story about a man
who becomes her lover
because he looks for a woman
like her but she can't be sure.

It's getting late,
let's try again.

The man in the story is a
writer. One day, the woman writer
meets this man, but doesn't know it's
he because they've never met outside
the story. This man talks without
quotations and moves without
verbs.

Carol Adler

They talk possible scripts,
a left-handed woman
who accidentally gets
trapped
in the mind of a man with no

ambition except to
go to the zoo, museum, Alaska,
alone—the story embellished by long
arguments, snatched coffee breaks,
a Bermuda cruise, God, how trite.

"What do you want?" he barks
as of course, she collapses in tears
and he rushes to the rescue, holding her
as she trashes him.
She grins. He grimaces. She
grimaces. He turns off the computer.

TRUSTING

There comes a time when tuna fish
      sandwiches grow hair and the mirror
talks back in brogue.
      Swinging by their tongues
in a foreign country

indifferent monkeys peel down
      intricate constructions, pausing
only to scratch themselves
      before soaped-up mirrors, parameters
suckle on waterproof
      pens, and on the keyboard
two horseflies play kickball
      with yesterday's crumbs.

At daybreak, the planet shivers
      and the sky opens in the East
to Venus and Jupiter, a single
      light. For the first time
in two thousand years, they
      reunite. In Rome, Adam stretches
an arm across the nave,
      Eve reaches out.

Carol Adler

Today, my love, I'm here
      forever, just you and me, whoever
you are, whoever I am,
      no bridge, no span. The phone rings as I
dial your number.

Duckling? Swan? I laugh.
      You grin. Never mind, the
words will come, their
      intention clear.

HOMEBODY

I enter the doctor's waiting room.
Musak, cold air.
        I have a manuscript in my briefcase,
someone's novel about unconsummated passion.
In matching chairs, between the magazines, a blue-haired
woman wearing a red hat, and her husband
(or a husband and a hat).
        Opposite, near the aquarium,
a pregnant teenager chewing gum, and a scrawny woman in
a McDonald's uniform who twitches her neck to the
Musak. Every so often she reaches into a bag of
jellybeans balanced between her knees.
        I look around, wondering which camp
is more palatable.
        Finally, I decide to stand by the door and start
editing. I am an alien, but I don't mind. A homebody who's
always at home,
        I have my work with me. The Musak
can even be one of the melodies the abandoned lover croons
to his absent beloved. Everything belongs.

Carol Adler

AFTER MAKING LOVE

I roll away from your darkened form

and fall into a seamless shoreline

stitched to the pale horizon

of another world

where water laps against

ancient stones and words stand like

monuments against a sky that reflects

their hieroglyphics *I am*, selfless and pure

as your blue eyes that hold the secret

to a charted route through that part of me

I permit you to keep

as map for the next journey

when again I shall need you

as star and cipher.

TEA AT THE EVERGLADES BATH & TENNIS CLUB

JET PATH

2 pm: the jet circles the island.
Below, aquamarine pools
glisten in the sun, lined up and waiting.

As when a person flies high enough to
transcend themselves they see the players'
instruments poised, listening for their cue.

Or when one lifts so high over the
past, patterns appear; coincidences
asking to be defined.

The jet speeds faster than sound, yet
nothing moves. I think we
must be on time, or overdue.

Carol Adler

MALAISE

Florida, like a damp sponge on
the forehead of an addict. Florida,
a swamp drained by the edicts of robber
barons, determined to build castles on sand.
Don't forget the pungency of first oranges,
saltiness of ocean wind, herons profiled in the rising
sun. Listen to the litany of rapes and break-ins;
notice the motorcycle gangs look away from
blood-shot irises, hold-ups at noon. Ask yourself
why there's no justice in a land that prides itself
on motherhood and apple pie, why the apples are wax,
mothers the slaves or victims of their own undoing.
Go outside. Steep yourself in the summer heat
'til it coats your skin and
seeps through your veins like mercury
in an indifferent barometer.

TEA AT THE EVERGLADES BATH & TENNIS CLUB

Ignoring the valet, I park my Toyota at the end of the lot

slip off my badge and straighten my wig.

Even though the trek through the desert

takes longer than planned, I'm still early

but the cucumber sandwiches

are already next to the samovars,

six penguins standing guard.

Why had I come—just to prove I could pass?

Even the chefs are Aryan. Hair bristles on my tongue, my

hands grow breasts. Two pigs squeal out of my shoes like

popovers, taking my toes with them. I stand nude in a

marble tub extending my nipples to the host. The mirrors

turn black. Is there some mistake, I wonder, as an angel

hands me a lyre. Psalms cleave to the roof of my mouth,

rosehips become blood. As I limp down

the golden staircase, the Red Sea parts

indifferently. Outside

I crawl on my knees over burning cinders.

WEATHERING

INHUMAN NEEDS

February splats onto the table opposite a large bowl of force-bloomed forsythia, as if to sit down with the Talmudist, If not now, when? Ignoring languaged limitations, never and no, imaging of stumps and hunchbacks: igniting the sun's chill with an Aquarian spark—as if this reassurance would automatically sprout green, The Winter of Dissolution canceled by ice cream, the penny arcade.

In spite of errands and call waiting, the more enlightened make a point of listening. Adapting to wind chill and rejection, shrugging off odors of fake strawberry and sheep, forecasts of condition. Meanwhile, circumstance saturates every pore, the baby squalling.

Perhaps it's better to do without than wait for a distant cousin to warm the palm: klesmers who drop their leavings on the most expensive lawn, singing as if Spring were forever, voices running in a running stream. They will teach you about equal distribution of bolts and funnels "in the name of Spirit," and how to con. Each month may have a different picture, but the seasoned hooker rips them off unthinking.

Carol Adler

On a visit to a new place, observations sharpen. Helena discovers the indoor pool warm and suitable for the prima ballerina, arrangements of forsythia and tulle for the Grand Finale. A band of light impenetrable and whiter than white serving to intensify purity within, to keep out the angry opportunist, sooty crusts. In time, salt will eat his heart out, leaving ugly potholes. She may pause to step daintily around them, or simply leap over, knowing that June is just around the corner.

THE REASON FOR METAPHOR

February in Vienna,
Bitter cold. Only a few snowflakes
worrying the panes.

Outside, twelve pigeons
are perched on the ledge
twelve porcelain replicas,
Hapsburg figurines from the
Kunsthistoriche.

Twelve cups
in the Emperor's pantry.

In the hallway
twelve portraits
of the Emperor
twelve of the Emperor's children
and wives.

Carol Adler

Perched on the embouchure

of a golden flute

twelve glass

nightingales.

Apple blossoms shower the air

as the concert begins.

AGE OF UNCOVERY: APRIL FOOL'S DAY

Someone must have turned on the light

or maybe it was just a feeling.

I woke to the sound of turtle-doves

not just cooing, but singing an intricate

Montiverdi-like madrigal. I know even the most gifted

conductor couldn't teach turtle-doves

to master four-part harmonies, or even

sing in unison. Birds are birds.

I'd like to dream in continuous swoon

knowing this wish is my only reality

like the reality in sex that seems to

intuitively seek hidden intimacies. Dreams

that force two souls to shed their separateness

zap, dropping them into a reflecting pool of

touch and taste that scatters the heart

forcing it to enlarge itself

in widening rings. I've scoffed at the lover

who spends his life trying to effect

a perfect orgasm, the addict who won't give

up until he finds the Truth.

Carol Adler

Armies have polluted their dreams
in order to purify rivers of blood
and return to the bed of love
with suitable charms. How many Crusades
ended up as ritual slaughters? Flashing metal
from sharpened blades pleasurably ripping
at flesh; convolutions of
maimed bodies rotting in the sun. "Amo, amas
amat" in tasteless wafers. Communion
of lips and tongue.

Monteverdi was no saint
nor can any artist control
his emotions if his lover steals
the key to his strongbox. We're only
human. Even turtle doves drop their excrement
wherever they can.

Perhaps Freud was wrong. Perhaps
we take pride in needlework, the tatting
of intricate affairs, lacy wristbands
of black adorned by peach-colored roses. Simple ticket for
immorality to anything that lasts
longer than a kiss, spray-painted initials whitewashed
from the mind.

I know the assurance I need each day

is nothing more than my own affirmation mouthed

in language my body understands: simple gesture

of peeling an orange, keeping the rind intact

without puncturing its delicate skin.

Carol Adler

FOURTH OF JULY

The giant kaleidescope is already revved up
      and set into position
      and we're ready to begin
once we've centered ourselves and started to spin

so it comes as no surprise to anyone except maybe
      the children
      that as soon
as it's dark enough to see the light

we hear the first sizzle and crack followed by
      fricative sprays
      that whistle and snap
producing peacocks, palmettos—prismic displays

that splat into the water and shoot up again
      in backward dissections.
      "All we need is reality,"
sighs a veteran. "At what price,"

grimaces his mother, testing the milk
    against her wrist.
      Grouped around the table
each Master signs with a flourish, blots and

passes the pen, glancing up only to check
    the Wall Street Journal
      and discrepancies
in a hidden agenda.

Shivers, palpitations. More light. More showers—
    and then—as we inhale
    and wait—exhale—
deep within: the First Vibration.

Hissing as it lifts its head,
    rattlers shaking,
    and rips into the sky.
The baby screams as it starts to uncoil

Light peeling from its skin and shooting up
    in blazing spurts
      that shower into a circle of stars
and stripes, lincoln, washington, flowers

that blossom then detonate.
> More crackling, more screams,
> another jet,

music from the band below.

When it's time for the Grand Finale
> all the popcorn is gone
> and soap bubbles blown

to vanishing. "But it's the spirit that counts,"

says the doctor, his laughter turning to
> ashes as the Masters
> remove their jewels,

their lace cuffs sliding back.

Inert wands lay on the cement in pools of wet.
> Only two percent got the message.
> It's not that freedom's too

difficult. It just couldn't be detected.

OCTOBER MOON

You were ready, you said, to heal the universe, because
now you knew about desperation and fear and rejection
and what it was like to be strung out on drugs
until you didn't want to do anything except look
for the next fix.

Sitting across from me, poking at
your salad, your clear eyes steadied on mine as you
poured out your soul. I wasn't attracted to you,
nor did I even listen to your shit, because I knew you
wanted money. You'd banked on a rich bitch from
Palm Beach and instead you got me.

After I paid the bill, I imagined you tripped
out of the restaurant over to Angela's or Andrea's or
Electra's—the name of your last wife, as strung out
as you—and spent the evening sprawled on the
floor smoking pot delivering more diatribes
about cosmic sex and synchronicity while the
women played with you and you braided their hair.
I imagine you wiped yourself with my
poetry or stuffed it in your shoes, or maybe
read it to one of your cronies at the Arts Bar.

Carol Adler

This morning when you called, I wanted to hang up
but we ended up talking for over an hour. You
told me how you'd sat in the tub with the razor,
ready to end it all, then heard voices that
commanded you to wait a minute and you
found yourself taking off to Gainesville
where you ended up in a cave for
eight months meditating until you saw before you
The Crystal City of your inner self.

You told me how you lost your license for
architecture, that you owe the government for
back taxes, one son is in jail, your psychiatrist
is a yes man ... Thank God for the clear vision
of you crumpled in a heap beside
all the filthy puke-streaked played-out
versions of yourself. Thank God for your beautiful eyes
pleading for help and for the illusion that I could maybe
turn you over to the perfect healer who would answer
the beeper even if it was Saturday and rush to your rescue
pulling you back to the age of four when your mother
came at you with a knife before walking out, leaving
you at the table, fork lifted.

ATTRACTING OPPOSITES

I was born in the month of the archer

the month of fire and ice

or laughter, the deliberate withholding,

planned extremity. So I know, above the

clouds, low ceilings, the clever one

still plans to come. It is a furnace, a

mouth of Damaen. And you who run from him

beyond the forest into the clearing, what

can you do about guilt? If the archer shoots

one swift arrow, be convinced

it will center not by aim but

speed and intent, straight through the

white shining.

LEAVING

IT WAS A LEVELING

It was a leveling that quieted the winds. It stopped
when thinking stopped, when the mouths clamped shut, it was
almost humorous, the sorrow drifting off, sympathy
canceled out. Though I can tolerate storms, they have
secretary claws, executive teeth, they push
into a place like a raging addiction, in no time
can decimate tomorrow's resolutions, scribbled agendas,
multiple forms. I was turmoil. I craved
attention, my love was conditioned.
I collected Methods, memorized the right slang, bought six-inch
heels. The truth that finally came demanded
long-term rejection, programmed safaris. This is
the heart that laughs and this is the heart that connects.
The eye on the forehead is only a lens. The winds taught me
this when they took me by surprise. I was dreaming:
I shoot up in bed, my body is shaking
I'm painted like a clown, voices
chant mantras, my books are gone, the door swings
open. I scream for my husband but
he doesn't know who I am. I recite
credit cards, birth dates. I say "Daddy," but he only
looks at me and asks, "What time is dinner?" reminding
me he's already famous and due before

Carol Adler

nine. On the patio, salamanders cling to
the fence, frogs leap against the door, jacarandas
rattle, inside the television blares war.
On the card rack none of the messages
are mine and in the movies all deaths have the same
killing. We're told to be happy without definite
instructions. We're told to swim laps to feel younger,
to wait patiently for the sirens.

LEAVING

I drive away from the house of myself
without records or books

as if on a five-minute
errand printer still running

head spinning from the shock
of his hand, stars tunneling from my head

I will not look back at the
silver box where the numbers are

gone from the name
I strip off. This crazy woman is no one

I've met. When she comes to the
door I will not let her in because I

will not be there but she doesn't know that
yet. Time it will take, to disconnect.

Carol Adler

LOCKING THE DOOR OPEN

Suddenly the door flew open.
Promises flew out and scattered over the streets
among gnats and mosquitoes that flew around
them in circles, landing on alley trashcans with the flies.
In front of me, rising out of the sewer, with wings
on each ringer, a tear-shaped form, trumpeting.
And the moon flew through the clouds.
Clock hands flew around their faces sweeping off crumbs.
A crow flew backward, like a misguided omen.
The dove flew without purpose, having memorized it before.
At my feet I could feel the lapis breeze
gathering froth, feel it swirling around me in the swift
undertow—a heightening, and spiraling
steam from the pits below,
where pigs roasted, their juices basting the flames,
squelching them only for a moment.
The rivers flew through the town collecting bruises, taking
them to the square where voices flew
among beggars and bejeweled madams whose poodles
flew at one another, as if quarreling about
something more urgent than food.
Everywhere one could see writhing bodies, barber poles
announcing tomorrow's fear, residue of plagues that flew

back and forth from one war to the next. Near
the Danube and the Keys, storks flew
over rooftops and made wreathes for little ones.
Eggs cracked into furred paperclips that waited
for directions stating there's a reason to speak out
before silence succumbs.
Affirmations flew through the wires,
and operators flew to their ears to receive them.
And the necklace of paper dolls flew into homes.
At once I flew to the front door and pounded.
Too late. It was locked open. Rattlesnakes
ran out from closets and drawers,
decisions dribbled and bounced, carpets
chased after me as I fought my way
back, but their tufted claws captured me
and scrolled me into the Law. I tried to kick
myself out, again too late. A metal belt snapped shut, I
was licked for postage, flipped into a bin. I tried
to cry out, but the questions were jammed
by a computer whose chips had been
stuffed into my mouth, a string of licorice
knotted over them. Words spiked my windows,
the glass shivered and flew to
the ground soundless. My vision blurred. I
saw myself beating against ignorance that

Carol Adler

refused to let me in. Once I thought I was
home. I thought I was mother. Now I know I
am dust, flying against this gutted openness, unable
to believe, unable to trust. Blinded by the Furies, I've
lost my credentials. Nothing matters except moving
forward when I know I am lost, moving backward
even if trapped. Here I am, a mummied tourist, handkerchief
apparition that flies in and out of a windy funhouse
whose painted door sings and rocks on its rusty
hinge, held there by an invisible host.

NO ONE

knew I was supposed to be dead
until I appeared as usual the next day

although the calendar had been trashed
so no one knew what day it was

that I was supposed to be dead. I appeared
as usual because I didn't know what day it was

although I didn't know the calendar
had been trashed. No one knew

I didn't know, nor did they know
I knew they didn't know. As usual

I was dead although I appeared
because I was supposed to.

Carol Adler

YOU, SILENCE

will not be disturbed. It's frightening.
        Even in mid-day nothing moves you, you
        stay rooted in the soil of yourself
as if you had nowhere to go except inside.

Is that true? And do you expect me to listen
        without your telling?
        Like a face in a storm
shimmering behind veils you wait

and I feel you drawing me
        toward you, into
        your ancient eyes—
what do you want?

REMNANT

everywhere the world has taken off
leaving me with missing pieces

time stutters in the brain
in clotted echoes

messages hyphenated
lines of construction

what was supposed to be
finished isn't even begun

my hands are ready
but my fingers are numb

in the pool i see remnants
of myself i could fill in
if i wished

but i know about
light
i am what i am

Carol Adler

RISHEA

After the amputation
I discovered Rishea in
the broom closet wearing
a bathing cap, goggles and pink orange
and lavender tights.
Gently I coerced her out and
invited her to attach her legs to
me so we could go around the
corner to a meeting
of minds. As soon as we
arrived however, I learned my
ego was up for grabs. Although Rishea
urged me to leave while I could, a woman in
back with no clothes on immediately
stood up and blocked the exit.
The room reeked
of fish and house paint and the
pain from my stumps qualified
as sufficient reason
to ask any questions I pleased.
But at the moment I couldn't
think of anything except Rishea
and how much I wanted her

to justify my need to be
recognized, in spite of my
handicap. Rishea said my
numbness was natural
because the power lines were
down. If she weren't here
inside me and if her head
weren't throbbing right
next to mine, I'd've gone
crazy by now. She's like mint sauce
for lamb, the plus on a report
card of all 'E's. She says if I
will it strong enough, my legs
will come back.

CARTE BLANCHE

One day, guiltlessly, the gods tore out whole months, even ate up conditions. Paperweights no longer made snow even though populations were shifting to Florida.

"What does hegemony mean?" asked Jesus, a seventh grader whose parents owned a used car lot.
"Who wants to know?" snapped the teacher, deliberating between ribs or pita. Perhaps, she reflected later, as she removed her pink bra and examined her tits in the sun, if he'd asked instead how it feels, I'd have said yes. No one seemed to understand.

Jesus cried all night, and the moon didn't rise over the ocean. But few were disappointed. After all, it was only the Fourth of July.

The School Board wanted to keep school in session year round, to save on power. But the State said it would ruin the beach tariff, so it was voted down.

By the time they found her, the teacher's body was badly swollen, but it didn't really matter, since the paper shredder broke and the ground was white as her gown.

DREAM

I knew it was time to wake up but
I wasn't ready. Soon the
hotel appeared, white ship,
immaculate, rotting clapboards painted
over. It reminded me of my little-girl
white leather shoes that my father used to
clean for me with a chalky fluid that
smelled worse than my mother's milk
of magnesia that never worked.
My father used to cover and dry, cover and dry
until one day the child disappeared.
When my mother gave up and shrieked "ENEMA"
I kicked and screamed, begging
for more time. One brush up against
my shoes and all the chalk would fall off
uncovering secret chambers, stuffed
cubbyholes, grubby finger marks on the
walls. Over her lap I went, as the hard rubber
nozzle was shoved inside.

The hotel had a screened-in
porch like my grandmother's, and it
was lined with pots of geraniums and

Carol Adler

there was a glider and rocking chairs
with striped cushions like hers. In the summer
we used to sit in the dusk and watch the fire-
flies come out and maybe listen to some-
one bouncing a ball down the
street or kids playing hopscotch, and
it was all so trusting and right, especially
when my grandmother emerged from the
pantry with fresh-baked cookies, sugar,
molasses, chocolate. She used to flatten them with
a fork, two neat criss-crosses like the railroad tracks
behind the hotel. On the cocoa box were tulips from
Holland like my grandfather planted
around the house. People said my
grandfather talked to himself but I
know he was talking to his flowers. The
whole yard was a garden and there was even
a vineyard. I must have said good-bye to
someone as I left the hotel.

The sun was bright. It was morning. Yellow-
hatted workers were digging ditches for
pipes and sewers and at some of the corners
the street signs were down. I kept walking
because I knew I had to. I also

knew I had to return to the hotel because
I was expected back. Yet something was wrong.
Where was my husband?
Surely by now he'd be waiting, surely it must
be time to return. But even though I thought
I'd memorized the
way, nothing was the same.
As if going in a circle, I kept coming back
to the yellow-hatted workers and I had to
carefully skirt around the mud that had
already splattered my stockings and
shoes. Then you appeared, my daughter, you
with your beautiful eyes and your understanding.
You took my hand and said, It's all
right, it doesn't matter. But it does, I insisted.
We have to get back. I'll know the hotel as soon
as I see it, it's wonderfully
old, just layered and layered with the
chalkiest white, they've done such a
good job. Even my screams are
hidden. And your father—we can't leave
him there with the marriage. Have you
heard from him? Surely he has to be somewhere.

Carol Adler

Why? you asked, as if to remind me of something
I'd forgotten. I awoke then, my tongue chalky, my
mouth dry, and soon after, you called, sweet
daughter, and I repeated this dream.
"Do you know what it means?" I asked,
over the miles seeing her blue eyes
gloss over like a summer storm.
"Yes," she replied. "Those
workers tore it down as soon as you walked
out. He's blocked, Mom. You tried."
Her voice was so like my own.

LIES

No trace of what happens until it's too late.

This morning the baby was gone.
It was nameless, I lied, glad
to see his relief. When we hugged each other
my love died. I vowed he would never know
he had become a stranger.
He doesn't like females, my body had said.
Embryos are holograms. The room was pink and blue,
the aura of healing bruises.
He didn't bring me home; he was busy.

Now I block out carnivals, playgrounds
and school crossings as I drive to that room.
Blood-brick buildings. A bleeding sun.
A man at a public phone calling
the hospital. A pregnant woman crossing
against the light. Each step another row,
soon the sweater will be finished.
Morning again. Steam from the shower.
With an impatient flick of his wrist,
he downs his juice and wolves All-Bran
on the run. Obediently, when his car stalls
I call the repairman.

Carol Adler

On Saturday my friends stop by, bringing
crystals and books, earrings, pendants.
The mail person dumps newsletters
from Peru about shamanism,
Greenpeace pamphlets, labels and stamps.
I'm safe here in suburbia. I don't even have
to cry. My mother left me her china,
my father his Shakespeare. I like people
even though he says they have too many
problems based on money.

Patterns so familiar
even resentment grows untended.
Slowly the world turns, each day
a little more. Though we embrace
and I feel my lean body against him
the truth is still there.

I knew where my heart was
and when he said no, I held on to it
like it was another lie about to be snatched.
Fait accomplis, I said firmly
as he advanced. My shoulders came out
to meet him with a needle.

GIFTS

My mother-in-law spoke English like I
spoke German and we both understood each other
through the bond of wonder and amusement that
I could bake her *linzer torte* and create
feathery matzo balls and *spaetzle* for her
"*boyle*"'s soups and stews. When

she broke up house, it seemed "not quite right"
to give all her treasures to
her "Marianna," so she insisted I take the Römers.
That summer, carefully we wrapped each
long-stemmed goblet in tissue and packed them
into the car. "Stay good together," she blessed
us, hugging the children.

When she died, the goblets turned to stone
but I didn't know that yet, since it took ten
more years for me to walk out of my marriage
asking only for those glasses, which her "boyle"
wouldn't disown.

Carol Adler

Thank God her German came through for me
and *Sanks Gott* my English delivered the message.
Each day I pull out a stone from my heart
and place it on her grave. With wonder
and amusement, together we toast
"*L'chaim,*"—"To Life."

THANK YOU

THANK YOU

First I would like to express my confusion for
all the wonderful accidents that were
deliberately estranged from
any and all significance just to make
sure the coffee would be hot and there
wouldn't be any mistake about serving real
butter. Of course you must have
guessed by now if you hadn't known already that
such truths are invincible as America
and home fries, especially with grits. It's
wonderful as always to recall the times
we've tripped together over our own popcorn,
thinking someone else was to blame—until
it finally occurred to us that if life
has to have purpose beyond watching television
we'd better see if our bathing suits
still fit and not listen to the thunder.

How wonderful, when fear was in its
prime, to recall how we used to sit glued
to our inhibitions, watching them manifest
themselves in carefully charted plane flights that
would later be Xeroxed by the public and

Carol Adler

placed on the back burner. We used to
say we wished we knew what we were doing, but
now that a few more holidays have come and
gone without any future beyond what we've already
encountered and they seem to be here
forever, we realize how easy it is to
forget the mustard and yield to the gentle
breezes of summer, at least until one of our
special friends reminds us how lucky we are.

And that's really what I'd like to say tonight
and every night, whenever there's a full
moon. Yes, I'd like to pause a minute to
acknowledge the fruit on the vine,
and to recall with you the vision of
truth lined up like soldiers or coke cans at
a well-managed service station. We were all
young once, and that's a fact. Let's not get carried
away. Let's be here, right now, for
everyone who needs us. And let's remember how
important it is to catch the clothes just as they're
coming out of the dryer.

AGENDA

Each evening's ambiguity, especially
when the newspaper doesn't come or
the computers are down, is no reason
to abandon the miracle of what can always
happen in the structured time between
now and then. It's only a matter of observing
the mind as it attempts to connect with
the process of dispensing with things no
longer needed: fenders, meat grinders, cut-
out cards from shredded wheat boxes,
tonsillectomies. When did we take down the
curtains and put up blinds—the year
the relatives opted for Florida instead of
an annual visit? Uncle Jack's heart attack
that we learned later was another woman
and only he went to Tampa, while Aunt Lillian
filed for a divorce before she took
off with her own lover. Certainly the reasons
for Teflon were to establish priorities and
make life easier. After all, "it's not our
duty" to expose what some thief of the imagination
is determined to snatch once we leave
room to bring in the rest of the problem;

disguised, as usual. How could we have
suspected anything, living so far away, and when
antagonism seemed to be the only entertainment,
climaxing in bedroom scenes that could be
heard all over the neighborhood when the
windows were open?

Who really wants to know whether or not we
iron sheets or sleep naked—We skip rope
with reality not so much to deny the process
of aging as to give ourselves another chance
to become one with the hyperbole of
ego that arranges itself in prismic displays
even when no one's looking. So in order to
avoid self-estrangement in the process
of learning, we put on music, the *Mahler Fifth*
or maybe *Die Flederdmous,* hoping to change
vibrations and eliminate another dilemma.

Or we suggest another trip to the
foyer where the lighting is less dim—
as if portion-controlled perception would re-
adjust the painting that inevitably hangs
crooked every time there's a storm. Sheep and
mountains somewhere in Turkey that was bought at

an auction to cover a crack. Actually it was Aunt Lillian who walked out. She had it all planned down to the last detail, even leaving enough money to pay for the maid and dry cleaning. But it's not uncommon to blame the other person.

Carol Adler

IT'S ONLY A MATTER OF

indifference before
anyone catches on, especially
when everything we always were is in
present tense at another time, say,
when we forgot to be thirsty until
we recall the forty
years in the desert.

Call it being centered in someone else's
dream or in that sensitive
spot between the eyes. Even death is
parenthetic, a quick
trip between semesters, one of those
times when the luggage got
lost and you're stuck without
toothbrush and bra.

Silence might
pencil in the most important appointments
that could still be canceled
though there's no way of
telling, especially if the power's
down. Somehow I wish

this moment

could go on forever, then

I'd never have to worry about

checking it out against

another. But now the doorbell's

ringing and the rolls have to be

warmed.

Carol Adler

BEAUTY IN THE EYES OF THE BEHOLDER

One would almost think it would be worth giving
up, if the value could be placed right in the middle
of the aisle, where people could trip over it and
force the clerks to come running with mops; except
for the embarrassment, since no one wants to deliberately
bird-dog on the abstract or leave droppings.
Yet it seems to happen as naturally as
apples and sex. Just now, for example, when
the doorbell rang, it could have been
anyone. Which is why we install special sys-
tems and leave the TV on. So the
heart responds, Is everything OK? without
knowing why. Emergencies such as a shirt and
no pants, or hair in rollers. Beauty on
billboards driven past and stored in cemeteries
years later after the children
are grown and one stops to ask, "Whatever hap-
pened to Grandma's twelve-foot thighs and the tiger-
striped bikini?" Glass held high . . .
Perhaps this is why VCRs are so popular:
Self-control is the art of denial—
an audience of one never hears itself

cough, and we can re-run ourselves as long
as the stomach holds out.

If only we didn't have to drive through it
daily, stopping for the usual
flattery that eventually parks us in
angles that have to be confronted. Once
we open the door we know we've had it.
Defense could be anything from Avon to Armageddon.
Only yesterday the street was loaded with
mattresses, but thank god we knew how to get
around them . . .
"Recreation!" shouts the anchor
man, and although we're told his lies
are paid for in overtime, we board anyway, and
leave the rest to the elements, where hopefully surrender
becomes beneficial. Then: sure enough,
as soon as we round the bend in the
harbor, there she is, with her crown of dollar bills and
Mona Lisa smirk scraped clean of bird shit. One of us is
bound to lean out and scoop up enough coins for at least
a small dish without toppings. As we said at the beginning, before
being interrupted, flavor is in-consequential.

Carol Adler

SONG: "OCCASIONAL TIMES"

The clocks are working overtime,
the inner ratcheting is larded up with the norm.
What in daylight was called gesture
has been swept under the rug.

At the zoo the monkeys seem programmed.
What brand of money buys love?
Or shouldn't comparison be in degrees,
arenas for airing everyone's conception?

And how does the simple branch of an oak
the diviner plucks explode into
geysers of money from semblances of
dreams? Please relate to the deliberate obscurity

that underscores whatever this landscape is
creating, the rehearsed lines it is mouthing.
Once they were purchased at a premium only
because they seemed wrong,

confusion breeding excitement, energy
palatable and unique. Now cottages are boarded up,
only slums are affordable, or the lot
next to the vacant school. Everyone's watching TV.

Usually time will ignore us,
though memories, like souvenir match flaps
discovered years later in a moment of need,
can self-inflict. Or, like right now, on

the Interstate, bumper stickers: I
(HEART) . . . coffee cigarettes sex
whatever happens to fit for the
occasion. In cloud forms, symbols become

evanescent reminders. Or listen: the
concertmaster is tuning us with strung cat gut
and hair even before the music has begun.
With Mercury in retrograde and postal rates

on the rise, it's no wonder black holes can erupt in
canned laughter of a sit com, like smeared
lipstick on a wine glass. It's easy to get used
to bottled conditions, especially if we can take

Carol Adler

the vinegar and can afford to put

them on a card. Come closer, there's nothing

to fear. Let's turn off the news and

talk to each other until the evening disappears.

ONE-LETTER WORD

ONE NIGHT STOP

In Danbury Connecticut I couldn't see
anymore it was raining
too hard and night so I
pulled up in front of
a line of dirty underwear
dashed out
and said yes to the Lebanese attendant for
"Room 213"

said yes to the eyes
that followed me as I ferried across
the sea of puddles yes to the man
dumbly sub-
mitting to fleshy lips

Spacious pristeen a moon was
under the bed
and a saucer of milk

I'm only visiting
I told myself
no one
cares if I play with

Carol Adler

him lick milk
from his balls no one
will see me get punished

but I kept thinking about
tomorrow and the clean bed
linen and my clean
nightgown I'd carefully packed
in the one bag that came in
with me and that also
had my alarm clock
and a poem I'd written
about love I kept

thinking about kneeling on the
stones and shrieking
while he ripped out my tongue
and placed before me
the vomit of words

there was a postcard in the drawer

with a picture of a wall and

people praying before it

with a purple pen someone

had scribbled "Allah be

Damned"

all night I could hear a woman

crying

Carol Adler

RIVER OF BLOOD

As it was meant to be
we came together to serve
the river of blood
that ran through the village
and was said to date back
to the Age of Miracles.

It wasn't long before even the
trees bowed down. Medicine men
lifted the curse by connecting
pure thought to Earth's
intention.

In the Spring, fish swam upstream
and we danced until dawn.

There were those who rejected
our mission. No wonder.

Stones grew cold in their palms,
our music only a buzz
in their ears.

Before they died
they turned on us, shouting
death was better than
fear.

The music grew louder.
We couldn't hear.

On the river banks
we collected their hardened tears.

Carol Adler

ONE-LETTER WORD

I.

The one-letter word bounces in its crib
It is tall and straight
Large-boned, large appetite
It is always hungry

The one-letter word learns how to walk
It walks through doors and the doors
Follow after it

And it grows taller taller taller
Now the doors bow down
They let it walk over them and
The whole house follows

The one-letter word learns it is a car
It learns it is a boat
It is impressed with nouns

At once the one-letter word

Makes a list of cities

It buys Pimsleur tapes and a food scale

It mimics, "Ego, ego, ego."

And the lawyers start calling.

II.

The cockroaches come out at night

Make a fist one-letter word

Tell the philosophers to go within

Tell the psychologists to heal themselves

In the test tube that is your stomach

In the computer that prints out your fate

You are reading surfaces

You the hamburg beholder

Your hands are cushions

Your mouth is a bone

You are a soup ladle a broom

Carol Adler

III.

Dance naked one-letter word
And your teeth will become horses

Walk on your warts like a martyr
Your feet will sprout compasses

Keep turning every question into tongues
Let the ark feed your psalms

Balance the light on your horns
The breath of the stars will rescue you

Only for a while will you be fooled
Thinking you can take what you already have

Only for a while will you wish
For marshmallows and a pink chin

IV.

Buy Mozart Kugel for the one-letter word
Fire the splotchy-cheeked preacher

And dispense with *should*
Snatch up carpets and drawers

Make aisles of lightning bolts
Commission statues and pretend
You and the one-letter word
Are competing for the Pulitzer

Use pleasure as the best excuse
For loving it
Don't expect miracles or bargains

If you do you'll end up signing
The one-letter word as your given name
And people will talk

Behind your back the doctors will line up
The creditors will be alerted

And every time you say you don't care
Or you're worth the price
The one-letter word will grow weaker

Carol Adler

V.

Humble yourself to the one-letter word
And you will cancel your indigestion
Even the lottery will seem possible

Close your eyes and
Lock the door open

Strap the one-letter word to your forehead
Wrap it around your arm

Surrender to the one-letter word
If you don't
It will tickle you until you bleed

VI.

Beware of those martyrs
They will pawn sticks and stones
As diviners and fetishes

Find the hospitals in their eyes
See them blindfolded
Reading the one-letter word

If they invite you
Bring your own food
Don't even drink the water

When they pass the cup
Smile and say you gave at church
Roll in your shadow before they step on it

If they call you for help
Refer them to someone more qualified
Unless they can pay

Beware of those martyrs
Their promises are tent flaps
Their pamphlets are treason

VII.

At last you can press the
one-letter word and get good reception
At last you can be anyone

The one-letter word
Is writing these words
And it can't even sign its name

Carol Adler

The one-letter word
Laughs at itself and knocks off
Its head without thinking
It likes to play games

Make love to the one-letter word
Your eggs will always be perfect

Make love
The one-letter word won't ever
Ask you to stop

CINEMA PARADISO

I'm thinking of little Michael who spent his childhood
    clinging to a pet monkey given to him by his dad
    at birth: thus, Michael's nickname, "Monkey." I'm
thinking of the day Monkey's dad announced he was leaving
    home for another woman. Monkey was seven. I'm
thinking of the way Monkey cried when
    Monkey asked his mom if he would ever come
    back, and when love died did it also go
to heaven. At twelve, Joey became Monkey's best friend, and
    then Joey was kidnapped and killed. His body was
mutilated and returned to his folks UPS. His mom went crazy.
    It seemed logical, thought Monkey, to join his friend
    so he rode his bike to the Causeway bridge and waited
    until dark.
At home, an eyeless lump of chewed-on Steiff lies inert on
    the bed and tries to remember the last words Monkey's
    father said. What had he promised? Ice cream? A trip
    to the zoo?

Carol Adler

SLEEPING PLANET

A heart is frying in the pan, its blood
hardening into a wax crayon that an American
cowboy is trying to shove into a golden pencil
sharpener. The heart died several centuries
ago but was freshly wrapped in cellophane
when the woman bought it earlier that day.
It was a mouthpiece for the ripped-out
phone at the corner and it still reeks of
the foul breath of its users, odors of
sweat and urine mashed into garlic. Desperation
and denial pour through the vents and
saturate the street.

Once the heart belonged to a troubadour
who wooed the miller's daughter, but
when she fell in love, he ran far into
the next century and left her with child.
He never saw his son until the little boy
became a priest in the mother's dream, and
swam out to find his father but he was
gone. When he called for help, his voice
drowned in the waves of his mother's
dream. Sometimes he still calls out

but now the streets are deserted
by five and the ocean is clogged
with shoes of the fishermen.

Where is the pure whiteness of a sun
that used to bleach those streets until
they turned to milk for the hungry
children? Where is the sparkle of sand
that used to whip up swords of
laughter, whirling them in a mad dance
of blinding passion that skipped across
the screen on lakes of limitless pleasure?
Tinkling bells, bracelets of enticing charms
or the clinking of glasses as lovers
toast their separate journeys into the same
fiction? Words, words.

The pale hair of the little boy is
streaked with broken promises. His feet
warp from walking the water-soaked boards of
the bridge that never seems to connect to
the domed portico where the angry priest
Elijah swings lazily in the hammock.
Oh, it is too much. As soon as he reaches
out for a soaked wafer it disappears in the

Carol Adler

mouths of icons that shiver and quake as they
repeat the same litany of age-old complaints.

He falls on his knees. The icons
fall after him, their hearts rolling out
of their cracked cases, rolling away
like marble. Bewildered, the lost child crawls
after them, his empty hands grasping the
light as his mother calls to him to turn off the
TV and come down for dinner.

THE MOST PROFOUND OF ALL MESSAGES

From "De Profundis" of James Wright, which was taken from the German of Georg Trakl

A cobblestone square, placard gleaming in the dusk.
A shul here once, Jews chanting "Yisgodol."
A marketplace, now only the words "Judenplatz."
The wind is chilly in this open space.

On either side, shops for hardware, gloves
handkerchiefs. Owners whose ignorance
keeps them safe.

Coming upon this spot,
a young woman is suddenly overwhelmed
by the sound of voices.

A bearded man, prayer book in hand
approaches and invites her in.
The wind whips through the wire fence.

Her heart starts to hammer.
With his diamond-studded cane, the man
lifts her skirt, fondles her.

Carol Adler

When she awakens, she is naked. Blood
streams from her mouth. A yellow badge
is dangling from her vagina.
Bells from the cathedral, voices
chanting the Mass.

DISPLACED

In Memory of Jerzy Kosinski - 1933-1991

He was already famous before he
made the headlines for twisting a
plastic bag over a head of cabbage and
filling the tub.

The head sank. Some said
it was a displacement problem. Others
that it was a matter of faith.
Still others blamed it on the recession.
People were sick of wieners and kraut.
Reasons are not important, states
the Society.

Although it sold more greens for a
week or so, the venture lost
six million.

Many take
their lives for granted.

Carol Adler

NAKED IN DAYLIGHT

Although it's only July
summer has already pulled out
leaving me on the tracks
still waiting to get on.

Why was I late? I'm always on time.
Unticketed, empty-handed

who told me to go naked in daylight
and forfeit the past?

In darkened windows
I see only your eyes
laughing at me

mouthing good-byes.

Carol Adler, MFA's first ghostwritten book listing her name as co-editor, *Why Am I Still Addicted? A Holistic Approach to Recovery*, was endorsed by Deepak Chopra, M.D., and published by McGraw-Hill. Other publications include three novels, five other books of poetry, and well over 200 poems in literary journals.

She has ghostwritten over 40 non-fiction and fiction works for a number of professionals in the education, health care and human potential industries.

Carol Adler

Currently, Carol is President of Dandelion Books, LLC, www.dandelion-books.com of Mesa, Arizona, a full service publishing company; and President and CEO of Dandelion Enterprises, Inc., www.write-to-publish-for-profit.com, a full service writing and editing company.

Carol's business experience also includes co-ownership of a Palm Beach, FL public relations company and executive management positions in two U.S. rejuvenation and mind/body wellness corporations, for which she founded publishing divisions.

She has served as editor of several poetry and literary magazines, and her career also includes extensive teaching of college English poetry, fiction, non-fiction and business writing, and conducting of writing workshops in Florida and New York State prisons, libraries, elementary, junior and high schools, and senior citizen centers. Carol has a B. A. in Philosophy and English from the University of Michigan, and a Master of Fine Arts in Creative Writing/Poetry from Vermont College/Norwich University.

Other Books by Carol Adler

Non-Fiction

Writers, Authors & Dream Weavers: I Heard Your Call For HELP! How to Write Non-Fiction, Fiction, Poetry, Memoirs, Children's Stories... and More (hard copy & ebook)

How To Publish & Market a Book Without Jumping Off a Cliff (ebook)

Do You Really Need To Write A Book? Tips & Techniques For Writing, Publishing, Marketing & Promoting YOUR BOOK! (hard copy & ebook)

Fiction

Come as You Are (by Sarah Daniels, a pseudonym) (hard copy & ebook)

Slouching Past Bethlehem (hard copy and ebook)

The Woman With Qualities (by Sarah Daniels, a pseudonym) (hard copy & ebook)

Poetry

Arioso - Selected Poems by Carol Adler (hard copy & ebook)

Jesus & The Tooth Fairy – Poems by Carol Adler (ebook)

Naked in Daylight (ebook)

Shaelot (Questions) (hard copy & ebook)

www.ingramcontent.com/pod-product-compliance
Lightning Source LLC
Chambersburg PA
CBHW031632160426
43196CB00006B/389